HELLO 2025 HELLO

VISION BOARD
Clip Art Book
FOR BLACK WOMEN

ADVENTURES

HOBBIES

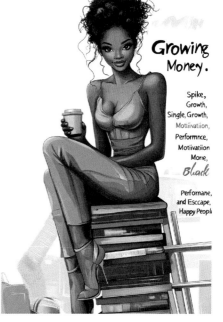

Growing Money.

Spike,
Growth,
Single, Growth,
Motivation,
Performnce,
Motiivatiion
More,
Black

Performane,
and Esccape,
Happy Peoplle

Black Queen

FOCUS ON YOUR
Progress
CELEBRATE
your wins

ACHIEVEMENTS

ACKNOWLEDGING
achievements

Believe and **achieve**

WORK
SWEAT
ACHIEVE

You Can Do
ANYTHING

Same
ME
Bigger
GOALS!

Celebrate YOUR
ACHIEVEMENTS

NO FEAR
NO LIMITS
NO EXCUSES

DON'T
QUIT

ALL
GREAT
ACHIEVEMENTS
REQUIRE TIME

 PRAY wait & trust

SPIRITUALITY

 Faith OVER FEAR

 Faith Endures All
 God's Love Never Fails

 Blessed by Faith
 Faith Fuels Hope

You are my CONSTANT SOURCE OF INSPIRATION

RELATIONSHIP

YOUR LOVE IS THE foundation OF MY LIFE

LOVE

I GOT YOU

FOCUSED
DETERMINED
unstoppable

BUSINESS

She DREAMS.
BELIEVES.
ACHIEVES.
I AM SHE IS ME.

SUCCESS
is a decision

Confident CORE

FUTURE
millionaire.

Believe
in
Yourself

Surround
YOURSELF
with
POSITIVE
PEOPLE

Work
HARD
SHOW THEM!

Live your
dreams, not
your fears

ready
FOR BIGGER
and
BETTER
things

Put
YOUR
ideas
OUT INTO
THE WORLD

MY DREAM HOME IS MY GOAL

AND I WILL ACHIEVE IT

WELCOME To Our Home

LOVE Begins AT HOME

HOME

this is OUR HAPPY place

Friends are the family we choose

FRIENDS

A good friend can change your whole life

BFF!

Love

Best Friends

family
IS EVERYTHING

FAMILY

you are
MY HAPPY
PLACE

SELFCARE

FINANCE

I AM STRONGER THAN MY EXCUSES

GYM

PERSIST UNTIL SOMETHING HAPPENS

WORKOUT

BELIEVE YOU CAN AND YOU will

WORK

BONUS IMAGES

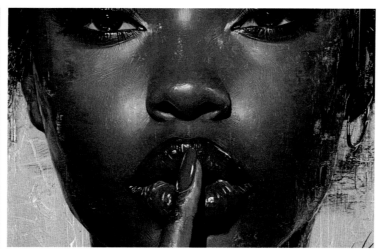

grow positive thoughts

Be pretty
♥ pretty strong
♥ pretty brave
♥ pretty kind

Be the reason
someone
believes in
good people

Be Kind

Good vibes

Priioriize your peace

Learning Intentions

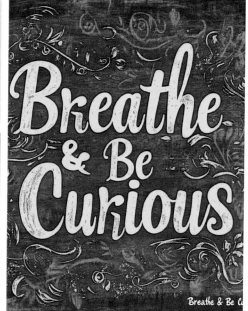

Breathe & Be Curious

Breathe & Be Cu

NEVER GIVE UP

Chase Your Dreams

Stop Thinking Start Doing

20

25

Focus on the goal.

LEARN GROW

Turn your pain into champagne

Thank you!

We are thrilled to extend our heartfelt gratitude for your recent purchase of our **2025 Vision Board Clip Art Book for Black Women**. Your support means the world to us, and we can't wait for you to explore the creative possibilities that await within its pages.

We believe that creating a vision board is an incredible journey towards manifesting your dreams and goals. With this clip art book, we aimed to provide you with a toolkit to make that journey even more exciting and visually engaging. We trust that the vibrant illustrations and versatile elements will empower your vision board to truly reflect your aspirations.

As you dive into your creative projects, we kindly request your feedback. Your thoughts are invaluable to us and to others who are considering enhancing their creative process with our book. If you have a moment to spare, we would greatly appreciate it if you could share your experience and insights in a few words on Amazon. Your honest review will help fellow dreamers make informed decisions and discover the magic of our **2025 Vision Board Clip Art Book for Black Women**.

And one more thing I'd like to say...if you find the books "**2025 Vision Board Clip Art Book for Black Girls**" and "**2025 Vision Board Clip Art Book for Black Men**" useful, you can find them on Amazon under the same author name, *Jasmine Eason*.

Wishing you endless inspiration and success as you craft your vision board masterpiece in 2025!

Warm regards,
Jasmine Eason

Made in the USA
Coppell, TX
06 December 2024

41917160R00026